Songs of a Wayfarer
and
Kindertotenlieder
in Full Score

Songs of a Wayfarer
and
Kindertotenlieder
in Full Score

GUSTAV MAHLER

DOVER PUBLICATIONS, INC.
New York

This Dover edition, first published in 1990, is a republication of two
works originally published separately: *Lieder eines fahrenden Gesellen*,
Josef Weinberger, Leipzig, 1897, and *Kinder-totenlieder von Rückert*,
C. F. Kahnt Nachfolger, Leipzig, 1905. A table of contents, lists of
instruments, and new English translations of the texts have been
added.
    We are grateful to the Bird Library at Syracuse University for the
loan of the score of *Songs of a Wayfarer.*

Library of Congress Cataloging in Publication Data

Mahler, Gustav, 1860–1911.
    [Lieder eines fahrenden Gesellen]
    Songs of a wayfarer ; and, Kindertotenlieder.

    The 1st work for low voice and orchestra; the 2nd for medium voice
and orchestra.
    German words; with English translation.
    Words of the 1st work by the composer; words of the 2nd by
Friedrich Rückert.
    Reprint (1st work). Originally published: Lieder eines fahrenden
Gesellen. Leipzig : J. Weinberger, c1897. Pl. no.: J.W. 894.
    Reprint (2nd work). Originally published: Kinder-Totenlieder von
Rückert. Leipzig: C.F. Kahnt Nachfolger, 1905.
    Words printed as texts with English translations on p.
    1. Songs (Low voice) with orchestra—Scores. 2. Songs (Medium
voice) with orchestra—Scores. 3. Song cycles. 4. Rückert, Friedrich,
1788–1866—Musical settings.   I. Mahler, Gustav, 1860–1911.
Kindertotenlieder. English & German. 1990.   II. Title: Songs of a
wayfarer.   III. Title: Kindertotenlieder.
M1613.M212L5   1990   89-755536
ISBN-13: 978-0-486-26318-2
ISBN-10: 0-486-23618-5

Manufactured in the United States by Courier Corporation
26318507
www.doverpublications.com

Contents

Texts and Translations

Lieder eines fahrenden Gesellen
(Texts by Gustav Mahler)

Songs of a Wayfarer

1. Wenn mein Schatz Hochzeit macht,
fröhliche Hochzeit macht,
hab' ich meinen traurigen Tag!
Geh' ich in mein Kämmerlein,
dunkles Kämmerlein!
Weine! Wein'! Um meinen Schatz,
um meinen lieben Schatz!
Blümlein blau! Blümlein blau!
Verdorre nicht, verdorre nicht!
Vöglein süss! Vöglein süss!
Du singst auf grüner Haide!
Ach! Wie ist die Welt so schön!
Ziküth! Ziküth!
Singet nicht! Blühet nicht!
Lenz ist ja vorbei!
Alles Singen ist nun aus!
Des Abends, wenn ich schlafen geh',
denk' ich an mein Leide!

1. When my sweetheart has her wedding,
has her joyful wedding,
I will have my wretched day!
I'll go to my little room,
gloomy little room!
I'll weep! I'll weep! for my sweetheart,
for my beloved sweetheart!
Little blue flower! Little blue flower!
Wither not! Wither not!
Sweet little bird! Sweet little bird!
You sing on the green heath!
Ah! The world is so lovely!
Chirrup! Chirrup!
Sing not! Blossom not!
Spring is truly past!
All singing is now done!
Evenings when I go to bed,
I think on my pain!

2. Gieng heut' Morgens über's Feld,
Thau noch auf den Gräsern hieng;
sprach zu mir der lust'ge Fink:
"Ei, du! Gelt? Guten Morgen!
Wird's nicht eine schöne Welt?
Zink! Zink! Schön und flink!
Wie mir doch die Welt gefällt!"
Auch die Glockenblum' am Feld
hat mir lustig, guter Ding'
mit den Glöckchen, klinge, kling,
ihren Morgengruss geschellt:
"Wird's nicht eine schöne Welt!?
Kling, kling! Schönes Ding!
Wie mir doch die Welt gefällt! Heia!"
Und da fieng im Sonnenschein
gleich die Welt zu funkeln an,
Alles, alles Ton und Farbe
gewann im Sonnenschein!
Blum' und Vogel, Gross und Klein!
"Guten Tag! Schöne Welt!"
Nun fängt auch mein Glück wohl an?!
Nein! Nein! Das ich mein',
mir nimmer blühen kann!

2. I went out this morning over the countryside,
dew still hung from the grass;
the merry finch spoke to me:
"Oh, it's you, is it? Good morning!
Is it not a lovely world?
Chirp! Chirp! Pretty and lively!
How the world delights me!"
The bluebells in the meadow also
rang merrily and cheerfully for me
with their little bells, ring-a-ring,
rang their morning greeting:
"Is it not a lovely world!?
Ring, ring! Pretty thing!
How the world delights me! Ho!"
And then in the sunshine
the world at once began to sparkle,
everything, everything took on
sound and color in the sunshine!
Flower and bird, the large and the small!
"Good day! Lovely world!"
Now surely my happiness also begins?!
No! No! What I love
can never bloom for me!

3. Ich hab' ein glühend Messer, ein Messer in meiner Brust,
o weh! o weh!
Das schneidt' so tief in jede Freud' und jede Lust,
so tief, so tief!
Ach, was ist das für ein böser Gast!
Nimmer hält er Ruh', nimmer hält er Rast,
nicht bei Tag, noch bei Nacht, wenn ich schlief!
O weh! O Weh! O Weh!
Wenn ich in den Himmel seh',
seh' ich zwei blaue Augen steh'n!
O Weh! O Weh!
Wenn ich im gelben Felde geh',
seh' ich von fern das blonde Haar
im Winde weh'n! O weh! O weh!
Wenn ich aus dem Traum auffahr'
und höre klingen ihr silbern Lachen,
o weh! o weh!
Ich wollt', ich läg' auf der schwarzen Bahr',
könnt' nimmer, nimmer die Augen aufmachen!

4. Die zwei blauen Augen von meinem Schatz,
die haben mich in die weite Welt geschickt.
Da musst' ich Abschied nehmen vom allerliebsten Platz!
O Augen, blau! Warum habt ihr mich angeblickt?
Nun hab ich ewig Leid und Grämen!
Ich bin ausgegangen in stiller Nacht,
wohl über die dunkle Haide.
Hat mir Niemand Ade gesagt,
Ade! Ade! Ade!
Mein Gesell war Lieb und Leide!
Auf der Strasse stand ein Lindenbaum,
da hab' ich zum ersten Mal im Schlaf geruht!
Unter dem Lindenbaum, der hat
seine Blüthen über mich geschneit,
da wusst ich nicht, wie das Leben thut,
war Alles wieder gut,
ach, Alles wieder gut!
Lieb' und Leid! Und Welt und Traum!

3. I have a glowing knife, a knife in my breast,
alas! alas!
It cuts so deep into every joy and every delight,
so deep, so deep!
Ah, what an evil guest it is!
It never keeps still, it never rests,
neither by day nor by night when I would sleep!
Alas! Alas! Alas!
When I look up to heaven,
I see two blue eyes there!
Alas! Alas!
When I walk in the yellow field,
I see from afar the blonde hair
blowing in the wind! Alas! Alas!
When I awake from the dream
and hear her silver laughter ringing,
alas! alas!
I wish that I were lying on the black bier,
and could never, never open my eyes!

4. The two blue eyes of my sweetheart
have sent me into the wide world.
So I had to take leave of the dearest place!
O eyes, blue! Why did you look at me?
Now I have eternal pain and sorrow!
I went out in the still night,
over the gloomy heath.
No one said farewell to me,
Farewell! Farewell! Farewell!
My companion was love and sorrow!
On the highway stood a linden tree,
there for the first time did I rest in sleep!
Under the linden tree,
which snowed its blossoms down on me,
there I knew not how life goes,
everything was fine again,
ah, everything was fine again!
Love and pain! And world and dream!

Kindertotenlieder
(Texts by Friedrich Rückert)

Songs of the Deaths of Children

1. Nun will die Sonn' so hell aufgeh'n,
als sei kein Unglück die Nacht gescheh'n!
Das Unglück geschah nur mir allein!
Die Sonne, sie scheinet allgemein!
Du musst nicht die Nacht in dir verschränken,
musst sie ins ew'ge Licht versenken!
Ein Lämplein verlosch in meinem Zelt!
Heil sei dem Freudenlicht der Welt!

2. Nun seh' ich wohl, warum so dunkle Flammen
ihr sprühet mir in manchem Augenblicke.
O Augen! O Augen!
Gleichsam, um voll in einem Blicke
zu drängen eure ganze Macht zusammen.
Dort ahnt' ich nicht, weil Nebel mich umschwammen,
gewoben vom verblendenden Geschicke,
dass sich der Strahl bereits zur Heimkehr schicke,
dorthin, von wannen alle Strahlen stammen.
Ihr wolltet mir mit eurem Leuchten sagen:

1. Now will the sun rise as brightly
as if no misfortune had befallen in the night!
The misfortune befell only me alone!
The sun, it shines on everything!
You must not enfold the night in you,
you must flood it in eternal light!
A little lamp went out in my tent!
Hail to the joyous light of the world!

2. Now indeed I see why you shower
such dark flames on me at many a moment
O eyes! O eyes!
As if it were, in a glance,
to concentrate utterly all your power.
Then I did not suspect, since mists enveloped me,
woven by beguiling destiny,
that the beam would already be returning home
to the place whence all beams come.
You wanted to tell me with your radiance:

Wir möchten nah dir bleiben gerne,
doch ist uns das vom Schicksal abgeschlagen.
Sieh' uns nur an, denn bald sind wir dir ferne!
Was dir nur Augen sind in diesen Tagen:
in künft'gen Nächten sind es dir nur Sterne.

3. Wenn dein Mütterlein
   tritt zur Tür herein,
   und den Kopf ich drehe,
   ihr entgegen sehe,
   fällt auf ihr Gesicht
   erst der Blick mir nicht,
   sondern auf die Stelle,
   näher nach der Schwelle,
   dort, wo würde dein
   lieb' Gesichtchen sein,
   wenn du freudenhelle
   trätest mit herein,
   wie sonst mein Töchterlein!
   Wenn dein Mütterlein
   tritt zur Tür herein
   mit der Kerze Schimmer,
   ist es mir als immer,
   kämst du mit herein,
   huschtest hinterdrein,
   als wie sonst ins Zimmer!
   O du, des Vaters Zelle,
   ach, zu schnelle,
   zu schnell erlosch'ner Freudenschein!

4. Oft denk' ich, sie sind nur ausgegangen!
   Bald werden sie wieder nach Hause gelangen!
   Der Tag ist schön! O, sei nicht bang!
   Sie machen nur einen weiten Gang.
   Jawohl, sie sind nur ausgegangen
   und werden jetzt nach Hause gelangen!
   O, sei nicht bang, der Tag ist schön!
   Sie machen nur den Gang zu jenen Höh'n!
   Sie sind uns nur vorausgegangen
   und werden nicht wieder nach Haus verlangen!
   Wir holen sie ein auf jenen Höh'n im Sonnenschein!
   Der Tag ist schön auf jenen Höh'n!

5. In diesem Wetter, in diesem Braus,
   nie hätt' ich gesendet die Kinder hinaus,
   man hat sie getragen, getragen hinaus.
   Ich durfte nichts dazu sagen.
   In diesem Wetter, in diesem Saus,
   nie hätt' ich gelassen die Kinder hinaus.
   Ich fürchtete, sie erkranken,
   das sind nun eitle Gedanken.
   In diesem Wetter, in diesem Graus,
   [nie] hätt' ich gelassen die Kinder hinaus.
   Ich sorgte, sie stürben morgen,
   das ist nun nicht zu besorgen.
   In diesem Wetter, in diesem Graus!
   nie hätt' ich gesendet die Kinder hinaus.
   Man hat sie hinaus getragen,
   ich durfte nichts dazu sagen!
   In diesem Wetter, in diesem Saus, in diesem Braus,
   sie ruh'n als wie in der Mutter Haus,
   von keinem Sturm erschrecket,
   von Gottes Hand bedecket,
   sie ruh'n wie in der Mutter Haus!

We would like to stay near you,
but it is denied us by fate.
Only look at us, for soon we will be far away from you!
What are only eyes to you in these days,
in coming nights will be for you only stars.

3. When your dear mother
   comes in the door,
   and I turn my head,
   look at her,
   my glance falls first
   not on her face
   but on the place
   closer to the threshold,
   there where your
   dear little face would be
   if you, bright with joy,
   came in with her
   as usual, my little daughter!
   When your dear mother
   comes in the door
   with her candle's glimmer,
   for me it is as always
   when you would enter with her,
   slip into the room
   behind her as usual!
   You, too quickly,
   too quickly extinguished gleam of joy
   in your father's cell.

4. Often I think they have merely gone out!
   Soon they will return home!
   The day is beautiful! Oh, don't be anxious!
   They are only taking a long walk.
   Yes, surely they have merely gone out
   and will now return home!
   Oh, don't be anxious, the day is beautiful!
   They are only taking their walk to yonder height!
   They have only gone on ahead of us
   and won't be longing for home any longer!
   We will overtake them on yonder height in the sunshine!
   The day is beautiful on yonder height!

5. In this weather, in this tumult,
   I would never have sent the children out,
   they have been carried, carried out.
   I could say nothing about it.
   In this weather, in this storm,
   I would never have let the children out.
   I feared they would fall sick,
   those are now vain thoughts.
   In this weather, in this horror,
   I would never have let the children out.
   I worried that they would die tomorrow,
   that is nothing to worry about now.
   In this weather, in this horror!
   I would never have sent the children out.
   They have been carried out,
   I could say nothing about it!
   In this weather, in this storm, in this tumult,
   they are sleeping as though in their mother's house,
   frightened by no storm,
   sheltered by God's hand,
   they are sleeping as though in their mother's house!

Glossary of German Terms

ab, off
aber, but
allmählich, gradually
Anfang, beginning
auf, on, for
ausbrechendem, erupting
Ausdruck, expression
ausdruckslos, expressionless
ausdrucksvoll, expressively
bewegt, animated, agitated, moving, *bewegter*, more animated
Bewegung, movement
bis, till, *bis zum*, until the
brechen, arpeggiate
Dämpfer, mutes
das, the
der, the, of the
des, of the
deutlich, clear
die, the
Doppelgriff, Doppelgr., double stop
drängend, pressing, hurrying
dumpf, dull, muffled
eilen, hurry
ein(e), a, an
Empfindung, feeling, emotion
Erlöschen, expiring
Erschütterung, strong emotion
etwas, somewhat
Figuren, figures, motives
fliessend, flowing, *fliessender*, more flowing
gänzlich, utterly
gebrochen, arpeggiated
geheimnissvoll, mysteriously
Geiger, violins
gemächlicher, comfortable, easy
gestopft, gest., stopped
getheilt, geteilt, geth., divisi
gleichschnell, at the same speed
(am) Griffbrett, sul tasto
grosse Flöte, flute
grossem, great
Halt, pause
halten, hold
heftiger, more intensely
hervortretend, prominently
höher, higher
Holzbläser, woodwinds
im, in, *im Takt*, in time

immer, always
innig, heartfelt
klagend, sorrowfully
klangvoll, sonorously
klingen, ring, *klingen lassen*, let ring
kurzer, short
lang, long
langsam(e), slow, *langsamer*, slower
leidenschaftlichem, passionate
leise, softly, gently
mit, with
muss, must
Nachschlag, Nachschl., final turn, *Nachschläge*, final turns
natürlich, ordinario
nicht, not, don't
nimmt, take, change to
noch, still, even
nur, only
offen, open
ohne, without
Rücksicht, regard
ruhelos, restless
ruhig, calmly, quietly
Saite, string
sanft, gently, smoothly
Sänger, singer
Schalltr. auf, bells in the air
schleppen, drag, *schleppend*, dragging
schlicht, simply, plainly
Schluss, end
Schmerz, pain, grief
schmerzlich, painfully
schmerzvollem, pained
schnell, quickly, *schneller*, faster
schwer, heavy, grave
schwermüthig(em), melancholy
sehr, very, very much
Sentimentalität, sentimentality
Singstimme, Singst., voice
später, later
spielen, play, *nur zu spielen*, only to be played
spring. Bogen, sautillé
(am) Steg, sul ponticello
steigernd, crescendo, increasing
Stelle, passage
stetig, steadily
Stimme, voice
streng, strictly
stürmisch, stormy

theilen, divide
Tones, note
traurig, sorrowfully
übermüthig, high-spirited
und, and
verhaltener, muted, restrained
verklingen, die away, *verklingend*, dying away
verlöschend, dying away
vorher, previously
vorwärts, (pressing) forward
weich, tenderly
wenn, if
wie, as, like

wieder, again
Wiegenlied, lullaby
wild, impetuous, turbulent
zart, dolce
Zeit lassen, allow time
zögernd, hesitating
zu, to (be), *zu 2, 3*, à 2, 3, unison, *zu Anfang*, at the
    beginning
zuerst, at first, at the beginning
zurückhalten, hold back, *zurückhaltend*, restrained
zurückkehrend, returning (to)
1., 2., 3., 4., 1st, 2nd, 3rd, 4th
3 fach geth., divisi in 3

Instrumentation

Songs of a Wayfarer

3 Flutes [Flöten, Fl.]
  (Fl. 3 = Piccolo [Pic.])
2 Oboes [Oboen, Ob.]
  (Ob. 2 = English Horn [Englisch Horn, Engl. Horn])
2 Clarinets (B♭) [Clarinetten in B, Cl.]
Bass Clarinet (B♭) [Bassclarinette in B, Basscl., Bcl.])
  (= Cl. 3)
2 Bassoons [Fagotte, Fag.]
4 Horns (F) [Hörner]
2 Trumpets (F) [Trompeten, Trmp.]
3 Trombones [Posaunen, Pos.]
  (Trbn. 3 = Bass Trombone [Basspos.] throughout)
Triangle [Triangel, Trgl.]
Cymbals [Becken]
Glockenspiel [Glksp.]
Tam-tam
Bass Drum [Grosse Trommel, Gr. Tr.]

> These instruments can be played by one musician.

Timpani [Pauke, Pk.]
Harp [Harfe]
Violins I, II [Violine, Viol.]
Violas [Vla.]
Cellos [Violoncell]
Basses [Contrabass] (At least some of the basses must have C-strings.)

Songs of a Wayfarer
Lieder eines fahrenden Gesellen

1 Wenn mein Schatz Hochzeit macht

A - bends, wenn ich schla - fen geh', denk' ich an mein Leid! an mein Lei -

- de!

10   Wenn mein Schatz Hochzeit macht

2 Gieng heut' Morgens über's Feld

gelt? Du! Wird's nicht ei - ne schö - ne Welt? schö - ne Welt!?

3 Ich hab' ein glühend Messer

Nicht bei Tag, — noch bei Nacht, wenn ich schlief!

4 Die zwei blauen Augen

Auf der Stra-sse stand ein Lindenbaum, da hab' ich zum ersten Mal im Schlaf ge-ruht!

Die zwei blauen Augen 55

Instrumentation
Kindertotenlieder

Piccolo [Kleine Flöte, Kl. Fl.]
2 Flutes [Flöten, Fl.]
2 Oboes [Oboen, Ob.]
English Horn [Engl. Horn, E. H.]
2 Clarinets (B♭, A) [Clarinetten in B, A; Cl.]
Bass Clarinet (B♭, A) [Bass-Clarinette in B, A; B.-Cl.]
2 Bassoons [Fagotte, Fg.]
Contrabassoon [Contra-Fagott, C.-Fg.]
4 Horns (F) [Hörner, Hr.]
Glockenspiel [Glöckchen, Glsp., Gl.]
Tam-tam [Tamt.]
Timpani [Pauke, Pk.]
Celesta [Cel.]
Harp [Harfe, Hfe.]
Violins I, II [Violine, Vl.]
Violas [Vla.]
Cellos [Violoncell, Vcll.]
Basses [Bass, C.-B.]

The 5 songs are intended as a unified, indivisible whole, and therefore in performance the continuity must be maintained (even by disregarding interruptions such as applause at the end of a number).

Kindertotenlieder
Songs of the Deaths of Children

1 Nun will die Sonn' so hell aufgeh'n!

60　Nun will die Sonn' so hell aufgeh'n!

Unglück, kein Un-glück— die Nacht—— ge-scheh'n!

2 Nun seh' ich wohl, warum so dunkle Flammen

das   vom Schicksal ab - ge - schla - gen.   Sieh'   uns nur

3 Wenn dein Mütterlein

Fließender.

Etwas bewegter.

4 Oft denk' ich, sie sind nur ausgegangen!

Ruhig bewegt, ohne zu eilen.

5 In diesem Wetter!

Mit ruhelos schmerzvollem Ausdruck.

Kleine Flöte.

2 Flöten.

2 Oboen.

Engl. Horn.

2 Clarinetten in A.

Baß-Clarinette in A.

2 Fagotte.

Contra-Fagott.

Hörner I.II in F.

Hörner III.IV in F.

Harfen.

Pauken.

Glöckchen.
Tam-tam.

Violine I
mit Dämpfer.

Violine II
mit Dämpfer.

Viola
mit Dämpfer.

Singstimme.

Violoncell
mit Dämpfer.

Baß
mit Dämpfer.

Mit ruhelos schmerzvollem Ausdruck.